Slither into the Untamed Realm of
SNAKES

Published by Wildlife Education, Ltd.
12233 Thatcher Court, Poway, California 92064
contact us at: 1-800-477-5034
e-mail us at: animals@zoobooks.com
visit us at: www.zoobooks.com

ISBN 1-888153-46-6

Snakes

Created and Written by
John Bonnett Wexo

Scientific Consultant
Richard Etheridge
Professor of Biology, Emeritus
San Diego State University

Contents

Snakes form one of the world's most successful groups of animals. They live on every continent but Antarctica and number approximately 3,000 different kinds, or species. Most of these live on or under the ground but some live in trees, and some spend all or part of their lives in the water. Secretive by nature, snakes stay away from people as much as they can.

The largest snakes are the Reticulated Python, which reaches 32 feet or more, and the Anaconda. The Anaconda is generally somewhat shorter than the python, but it weighs almost twice as much. It's estimated that at a record size, an Anaconda might weigh as much as 500 or 600 pounds. The oldest snake on record was a Boa Constrictor that lived 40 years 3 months 14 days at the Philadelphia Zoo. It's possible that older and larger snakes may live in the world's hidden places. But it's doubtful that there is a snake shorter than the rarely seen Thread Snake—a primitive snake that reaches about 4 inches.

Most snakes are brightly colored and come in a variety of patterns that often help them blend into their surroundings. The bold designs of the Rhinoceros Viper and the Gaboon Viper disappear into the leaf litter on the forest floor. The brilliant green of the Green Vine Snake harmonizes with the green of the rain forest. Many snakes are poisonous, many are not, and all play an important role in nature. When you learn about snakes you discover how interesting they are. Snakes are also some of the most beautiful creatures on earth.

ROUGH-SCALED BUSH VIPER
Atheris hispidus

FOREST COBRA
Naja melanoleuca

CALIFORNIA MOUNTAIN
KINGSNAKE
Lampropeltis zonata

GRAY-BANDED KINGSNAKE
Lampropeltis mexicana

ATTACKING
PYGMY RATTLESNAKE
Sistrurus miliarius

RETICULATED PYTHON
Python reticulatus

PERUVIAN OR
RED-TAILED BOA
Boa constrictor ortonii

EAST AFRICAN GREEN MAMBA
Dendroaspis angusticeps

PARADISE FLYING SNAKE
Chrysopelea paradisi

MANGROVE SNAKE
Boiga dendrophila

NORTHERN COPPERHEAD
Agkistrodon contortrix mokasen

BANDED KRAIT
Bungarus fasciatus
AND HATCHING YOUNG

RHINOCEROS VIPER
Bitis nasicornis

THREAD SNAKE
Leptotyphlops bilineata

7

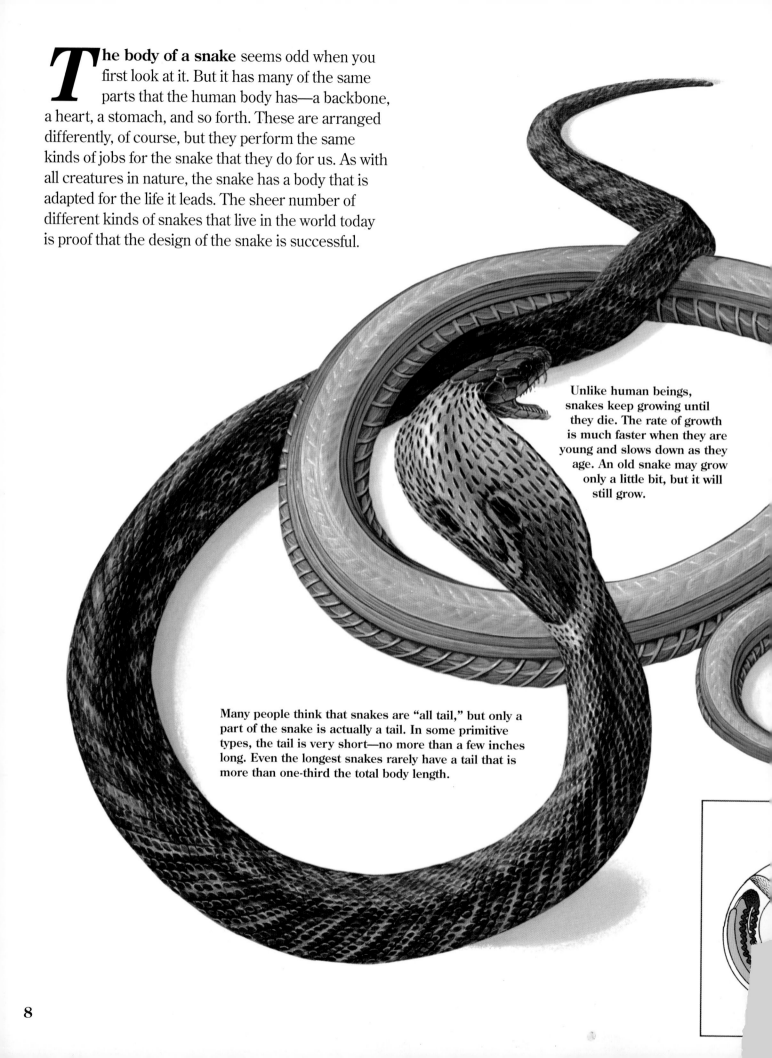

The body of a snake seems odd when you first look at it. But it has many of the same parts that the human body has—a backbone, a heart, a stomach, and so forth. These are arranged differently, of course, but they perform the same kinds of jobs for the snake that they do for us. As with all creatures in nature, the snake has a body that is adapted for the life it leads. The sheer number of different kinds of snakes that live in the world today is proof that the design of the snake is successful.

Unlike human beings, snakes keep growing until they die. The rate of growth is much faster when they are young and slows down as they age. An old snake may grow only a little bit, but it will still grow.

Many people think that snakes are "all tail," but only a part of the snake is actually a tail. In some primitive types, the tail is very short—no more than a few inches long. Even the longest snakes rarely have a tail that is more than one-third the total body length.

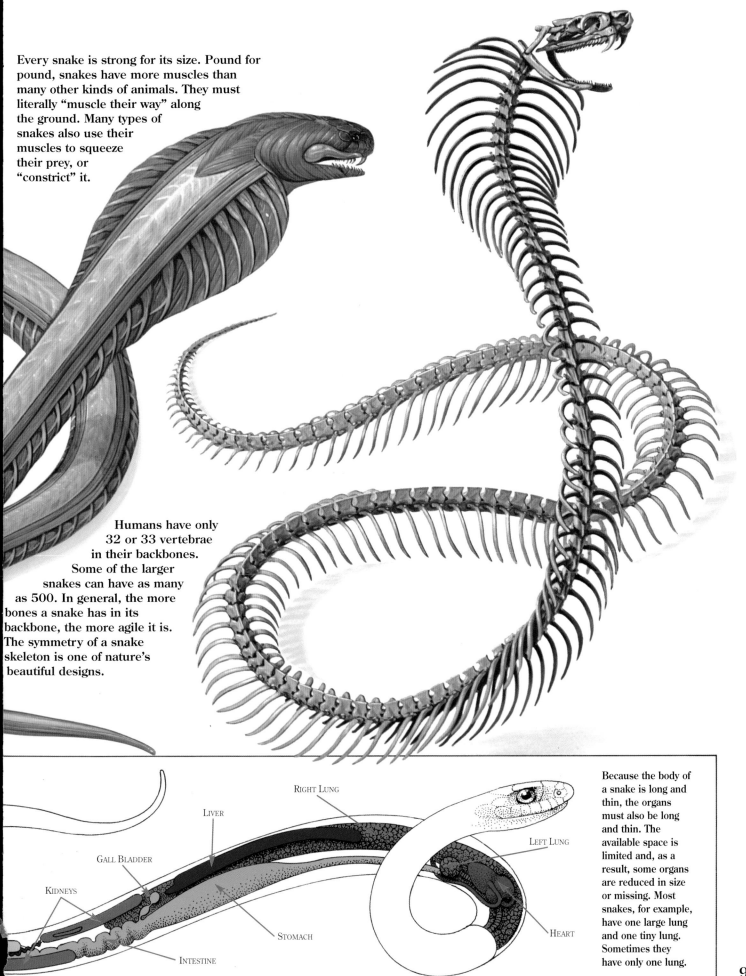

Every snake is strong for its size. Pound for pound, snakes have more muscles than many other kinds of animals. They must literally "muscle their way" along the ground. Many types of snakes also use their muscles to squeeze their prey, or "constrict" it.

Humans have only 32 or 33 vertebrae in their backbones. Some of the larger snakes can have as many as 500. In general, the more bones a snake has in its backbone, the more agile it is. The symmetry of a snake skeleton is one of nature's beautiful designs.

RIGHT LUNG

LIVER

GALL BLADDER

KIDNEYS

LEFT LUNG

STOMACH

HEART

INTESTINE

Because the body of a snake is long and thin, the organs must also be long and thin. The available space is limited and, as a result, some organs are reduced in size or missing. Most snakes, for example, have one large lung and one tiny lung. Sometimes they have only one lung.

The **skin of a snake** is important to the survival of the animal in many ways. The hard scales protect the inside of the body from injury. The colors and patterns that are part of the skin may help to hide the snake from danger—or they may warn predators away. As the snake grows larger, it sheds the outer part of its skin to make room for its larger body. (A young, rapidly growing snake may shed its skin more than seven times in one year.)

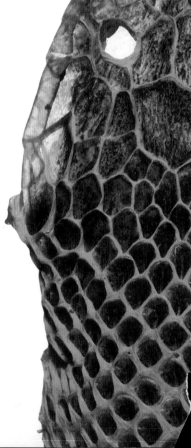

Snake skin has three layers. Only the outer, thinnest layer is peeled away when the snake sheds. The middle layer grows a new outer layer to take the place of the shed skin. The scales are thickened parts of the middle and lower layers, and they are never shed. The bottom layer contains the color of the skin, which shows through the upper two layers.

Snakes are not slimy. Their skin is hard and glossy, which reduces friction as the snake slides over the ground.

When a snake stretches, you can see that the scales are really "bumps" in the skin.

When a snake is ready to shed, its skin loses its shiny luster. The eyes cloud over and the snake becomes partly blind.

Usually, the scales on a snake's head are larger than the scales on the body. Head scale patterns are unique for some species and are sometimes used for identification.

The eyes of snakes are covered by thin transparent scales called spectacles, or *brilles*. These are shed along with the skin and the snake must grow new ones.

HOW A SNAKE GETS OUT OF ITS SKIN

Then, by rippling the muscles of its body, the snake stretches the outer layer of skin and begins to wriggle out of it.

The snake begins by rubbing its head against something hard until the skin splits open.

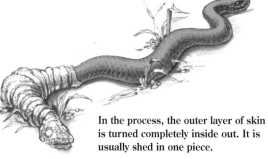

In the process, the outer layer of skin is turned completely inside out. It is usually shed in one piece.

Scales can take strange shapes. Some vipers, like this rhinoceros viper, have scales that look like horns on their heads. These "horns" help to camouflage the outline of the snake's head, helping the snake to hide.

Sometimes, snakes may gain a great advantage by looking like other snakes. This could help to protect them from predators. When a predator attacks a mildly poisonous snake, it often receives a painful bite. As a result, it learns not to attack a snake of a particular color or similar appearance. Therefore, non-poisonous and highly poisonous snakes with patterns similar to the mildly poisonous snake both benefit by being safer from that particular predator. It does little good for a snake to look like a highly poisonous snake, because predators that attack such snakes rarely live long enough to learn to stay away from them!

Scales on different kinds of snakes are different shapes. Some have ridges, or keels, running down the center.

This young Emerald Tree Boa is just beginning to turn green. Juveniles and subadults are orange!

Colors that seem quite bright may actually serve to hide a snake. In the lush tropical forest, bright green can blend into the background very well.

Dull colors and geometric patterns disguise the shape of a snake against certain backgrounds. Desert snakes often increase the effectiveness of their camouflage by burying themselves in the sand.

On the underside of a snake, the scales are usually larger and thicker than those on the rest of the body. These scales sometimes help the snake to move over the ground.

11

Getting around without legs is not as difficult as you might think. All snakes have at least three ways to move their bodies—and some have even more ways than that. Without stopping for a minute to worry about legs, snakes climb trees, swim, and go almost anywhere they like. A few species in Southeast Asia even glide through the air!

Rest easy. There is no snake on earth fast enough to catch a running human being. But be aware that some snakes can strike a fair distance and others can launch themselves through the air.

Scientists tell us that the ancestors of today's snakes had legs, but when they began to burrow in the ground, legs got in the way. Some boas and pythons, which are rather primitive types of snakes, still have small spurs on their bodies—all that is left of their ancestors' legs.

Lateral, or *serpentine*, motion is the most common way of moving for all snakes. To move forward, a snake pushes sideways against rocks, sticks, and other objects it finds on the ground. By doing this, the snake is able to "get a grip" on the ground at several places along the length of its body.

Using the muscles attached to each of its ribs, the snake then pushes each set of ribs against each gripping point, starting with the ribs nearest its head and working back toward its tail. As each set of ribs "pushes" in turn, the snake moves forward.

Caterpillar motion, another common method of moving, makes use of the large belly scales, or scutes, that most snakes have. First, the muscles that attach the snake's ribs to its skin are tightened **①**, pulling up the scutes and drawing them forward. Then another set of muscles **②** is tightened, and the first set is

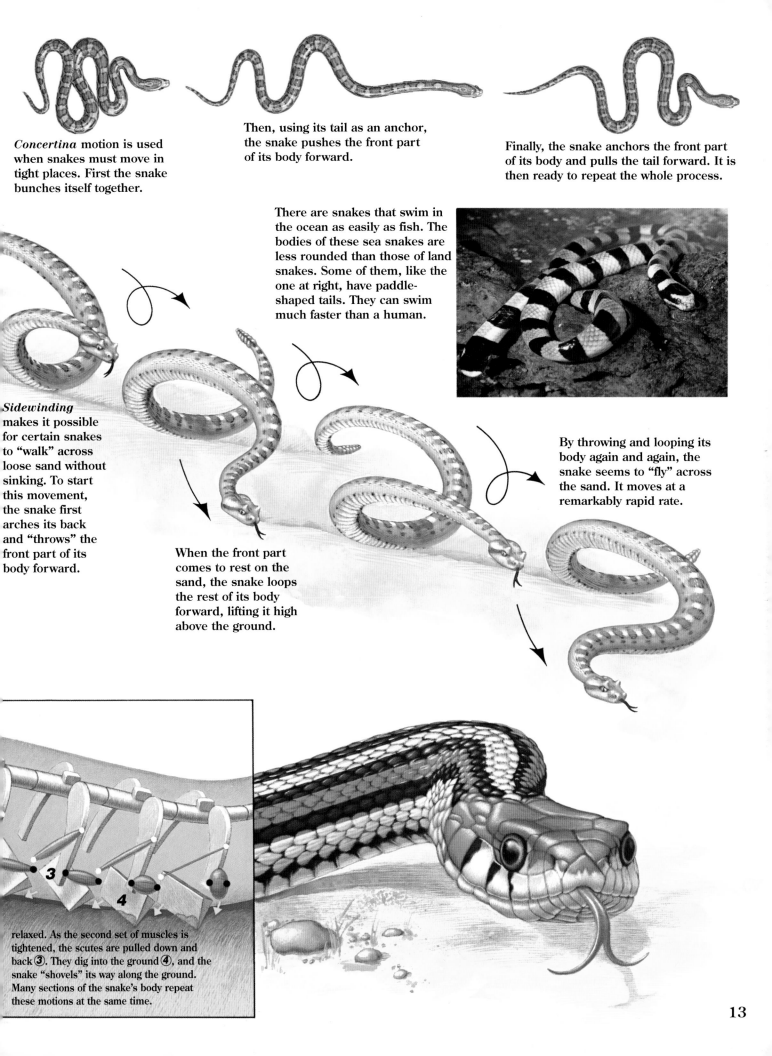

Concertina motion is used when snakes must move in tight places. First the snake bunches itself together.

Then, using its tail as an anchor, the snake pushes the front part of its body forward.

Finally, the snake anchors the front part of its body and pulls the tail forward. It is then ready to repeat the whole process.

There are snakes that swim in the ocean as easily as fish. The bodies of these sea snakes are less rounded than those of land snakes. Some of them, like the one at right, have paddle-shaped tails. They can swim much faster than a human.

Sidewinding makes it possible for certain snakes to "walk" across loose sand without sinking. To start this movement, the snake first arches its back and "throws" the front part of its body forward.

When the front part comes to rest on the sand, the snake loops the rest of its body forward, lifting it high above the ground.

By throwing and looping its body again and again, the snake seems to "fly" across the sand. It moves at a remarkably rapid rate.

relaxed. As the second set of muscles is tightened, the scutes are pulled down and back ③. They dig into the ground ④, and the snake "shovels" its way along the ground. Many sections of the snake's body repeat these motions at the same time.

Snakes are meat eaters, and they have effective ways to find and catch their supper. In general, snakes do not chase after their prey, but prefer to surprise it—either by sneaking up on it or by lying hidden until the unsuspecting prey comes close enough to be grabbed.

In many cases, snakes eat animals that humans consider pests, such as rats, and so the quiet efficiency of the snake as a hunter is often good for us. Even poisonous snakes do far more good than harm for mankind.

Most snakes have poor eyesight. Usually, they only see prey if it moves. They have no eyelids and cannot blink their eyes. This is why they always seem to be "staring"—even when asleep.

As a group, snakes eat a wide variety of animals and insects. But there are also many animals that hunt snakes. Their enemies include other snakes. Below, a kingsnake attacks a rattlesnake.

The hearing of snakes is not very good, and they seldom make use of it in finding their prey. They have no outer ear, so sound must travel by way of the jawbone to reach the inner ear.

Tricks are sometimes used to attract prey. This Southern Copperhead wiggles its bright yellow tail to hold the frog's attention, while the front end of the snake gets into position to strike.

Constriction is used by many types of snakes to subdue their prey. The snake simply wraps itself around an animal and squeezes hard enough to keep the animal from breathing. When the animal has stopped breathing, the snake must swallow it whole—snake teeth are no good for chewing.

The jaws of most snakes are only loosely connected to each other, so the snake's mouth can be opened very wide. It is even possible for a snake to swallow something that is wider than its own head. After a big meal, snakes may go for a long time without eating again. One snake survived for two years on one meal!

Some types of snakes have sensitive heat detectors that make it possible for them to locate their prey in the dark. Deep openings, or pits, between the nostril and the eye pick up heat given off by warm-blooded animals and tell the snake where the prey is hiding. Rattlesnakes and other snakes that have this ability are known as *pit vipers*.

Some snakes live almost entirely on a diet of eggs. They are able to swallow an egg whole, and may even swallow several large eggs at a time.

Snakes do not sting with their tongues. To make up for their poor eyesight, they use their tongues to help them smell what's going on in the world around them. By flicking the tongue in and out constantly, they pick up small specks of dust from the air and ground. These are carried into the mouth and placed in sensory detectors called Jacobson's organs. The "taste" or "smell" of the specks tells the snake what animals are near.

Inside its throat, an egg-eating snake has sharp bones that cut eggs open as they are swallowed. The egg's contents slide down the throat, while the crushed eggshell is pushed back out of the mouth.

Many snakes can swallow animals that are almost as big as they are. This means that the largest snakes can swallow BIG animals. Record books tell us of an African Rock Python (weighing no more than 140 pounds) that swallowed an animal that weighed more than 130 pounds!

Poisonous snakes use venom because it is a good way to capture prey. There is no need for a poisonous snake to spend hours and a great deal of energy squeezing its prey, and there is no need for it to chase after prey. The snake simply injects its venom and waits for it to take effect.

Of the approximately 3,000 different kinds of snakes in the world, only about 400 are poisonous to some degree. Of these, fewer than 50 are really dangerous to man. The rest are either too timid to attack people or they do not inject enough venom to do much harm. Some of the snakes that are most dangerous to people are shown here.

Rear-fanged snakes have rather small fangs. These are so far back in the mouth that the snake must really get its mouth around something before the fangs can do their job. The fangs are U-shaped (as shown), and instead of injecting venom they merely channel it.

It was long thought that rear-fanged snakes were not dangerous to people, and in most cases they are not. The Boomslang, above, is a rear-fanged snake, but its fangs are farther forward than other rear-fanged snakes. The venom from this snake can kill a person. Karl P. Schmidt, a famous herpetologist, died from the bite of a Boomslang.

The largest of all venomous snakes is the King Cobra. It sometimes grows to a length of more than 18 feet.

Black Mambas are probably the most dangerous snakes in Africa. These long and thin snakes can move very fast and can inject enough venom to kill 10 men.

The venom of Saw-scaled Vipers is particularly toxic to man. Even when it is only 10 inches long, this snake has enough venom to kill.

Front-fanged snakes, including the Coral Snake, at right, have fangs in a better position to deliver a dose of venom than do rear-fanged snakes. The fangs are still rather small, but they are rounded enough to inject venom more efficiently.

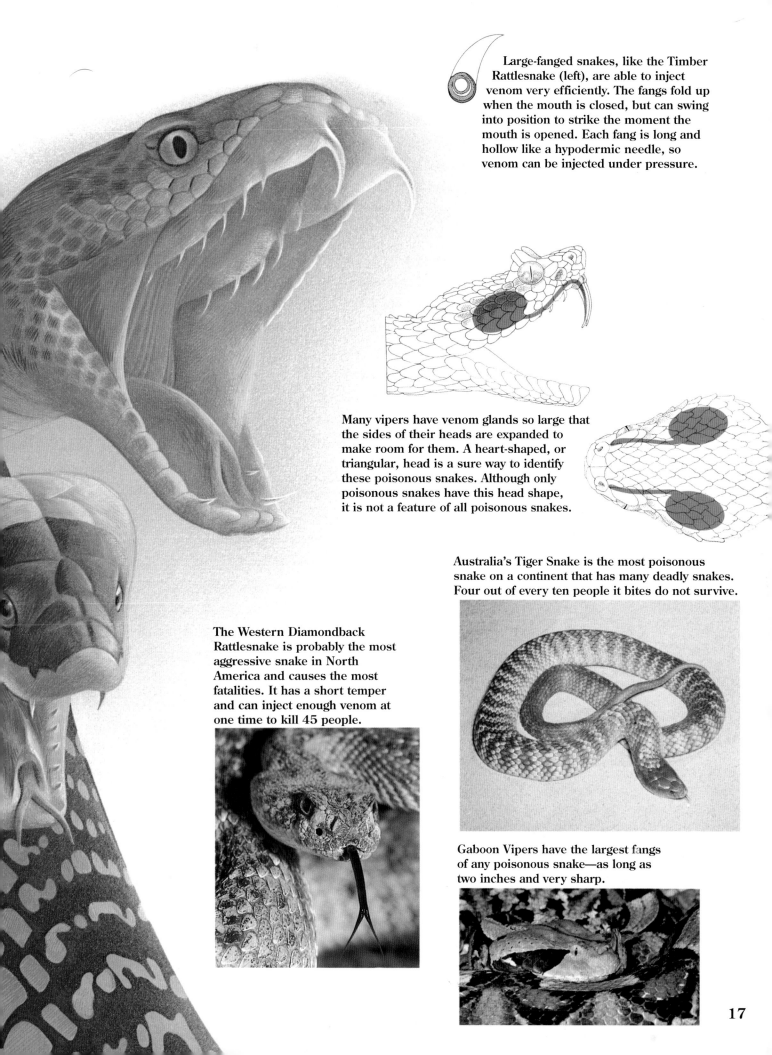

Large-fanged snakes, like the Timber Rattlesnake (left), are able to inject venom very efficiently. The fangs fold up when the mouth is closed, but can swing into position to strike the moment the mouth is opened. Each fang is long and hollow like a hypodermic needle, so venom can be injected under pressure.

Many vipers have venom glands so large that the sides of their heads are expanded to make room for them. A heart-shaped, or triangular, head is a sure way to identify these poisonous snakes. Although only poisonous snakes have this head shape, it is not a feature of all poisonous snakes.

Australia's Tiger Snake is the most poisonous snake on a continent that has many deadly snakes. Four out of every ten people it bites do not survive.

The Western Diamondback Rattlesnake is probably the most aggressive snake in North America and causes the most fatalities. It has a short temper and can inject enough venom at one time to kill 45 people.

Gaboon Vipers have the largest fangs of any poisonous snake—as long as two inches and very sharp.

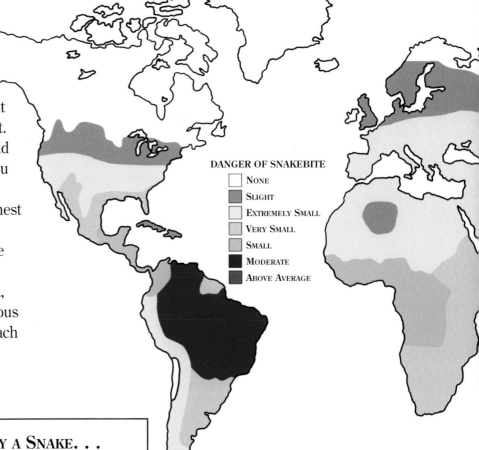

Snakes don't want to poison you. Their venom is intended for catching prey, and they would rather not waste it on an animal (you) that they cannot eat. In most parts of the world you can avoid being bitten by a poisonous snake if you will take just a few simple precautions.

As the map (at right) shows, the highest fatalities from snakebite occur where many varieties of poisonous snakes live near people and where medical care is often not available. In India and Burma, where there are many kinds of venomous snakes, more than 18,000 people die each year from snakebite.

DANGER OF SNAKEBITE

- NONE
- SLIGHT
- EXTREMELY SMALL
- VERY SMALL
- SMALL
- MODERATE
- ABOVE AVERAGE

In the United States, fewer than 10 people are killed each year by snakes. (About 115 are killed *every day* in highway accidents.) There are places where the death rate is much higher but snakebite is not really a major cause of death anywhere. Worldwide, only 1 out of every 115,000 people is killed each year by snakebite.

TO AVOID BEING BITTEN BY A SNAKE. . .

DO prepare yourself before going into areas where poisonous snakes live. Read about the kinds of snakes you may find so you will recognize dangerous snakes when you see them

 DO NOT go into snake country unless you are properly dressed. Wear heavy leather high-top boots and loose-fitting pants. Let the cuffs of the pants hang outside the boots.

DO NOT make sudden moves if you see a poisonous snake or hear a rattling sound. Snakes cannot see you as well if you don't move too much. Be careful you don't back away from one snake and run into another nearby.

 DO NOT sleep on the ground. You may roll over on a snake while asleep—or a snake may crawl in next to you to get warm!

DO NOT reach or step into places before you can see clearly if snakes are hiding there. Never reach over your head while climbing, unless you can see where your hand is going. Look over logs before you step over them.

IF YOU ARE BITTEN . . .

DO NOT PANIC! Be sure the snake has actually sunk its fangs into you and be sure it is a poisonous snake. Many times, snakes will not use their fangs or will not inject poison—and many people have been "poisoned" by perfectly harmless snakes. DO NOT try to catch the snake, because it may bite you again. DO try to get a good look at it.

 DO NOT try to treat the wound yourself unless it is absolutely impossible to get to a doctor quickly. By trying to treat a snakebite, many people do more damage to themselves than the snake has done.

DO get to a doctor as quickly as you can, but DO NOT run. Physical exertion causes the heart to pump blood faster and will make the poison spread faster.

Snakes do a variety of things when they try to scare an intruder away. Most of them hiss loudly, and many—like the Boomslang (at right)—inflate the throat and neck region. This makes them look larger and more dangerous.

When a snake shows you the inside of its mouth and the lining is brightly colored, move away. The snake is very likely to be poisonous.

If an intruder does not scare easily, some snakes, like this Hognose snake, will "play dead." The intruder may then lose interest. Do not touch a snake that looks dead. Even a non-poisonous snake can give a nasty bite.

The only use that a rattlesnake has for its rattle is to scare away animals that it doesn't want to kill. When it hunts, the rattle remains silent so the prey won't be warned of the rattler's approach. The sound of a rattle can often be heard up to 60 feet away.

When a person and a snake meet, the snake usually tries to get away. If the snake is cornered and can't get away, or if an intruder surprises it, that is when the snake will usually bite.

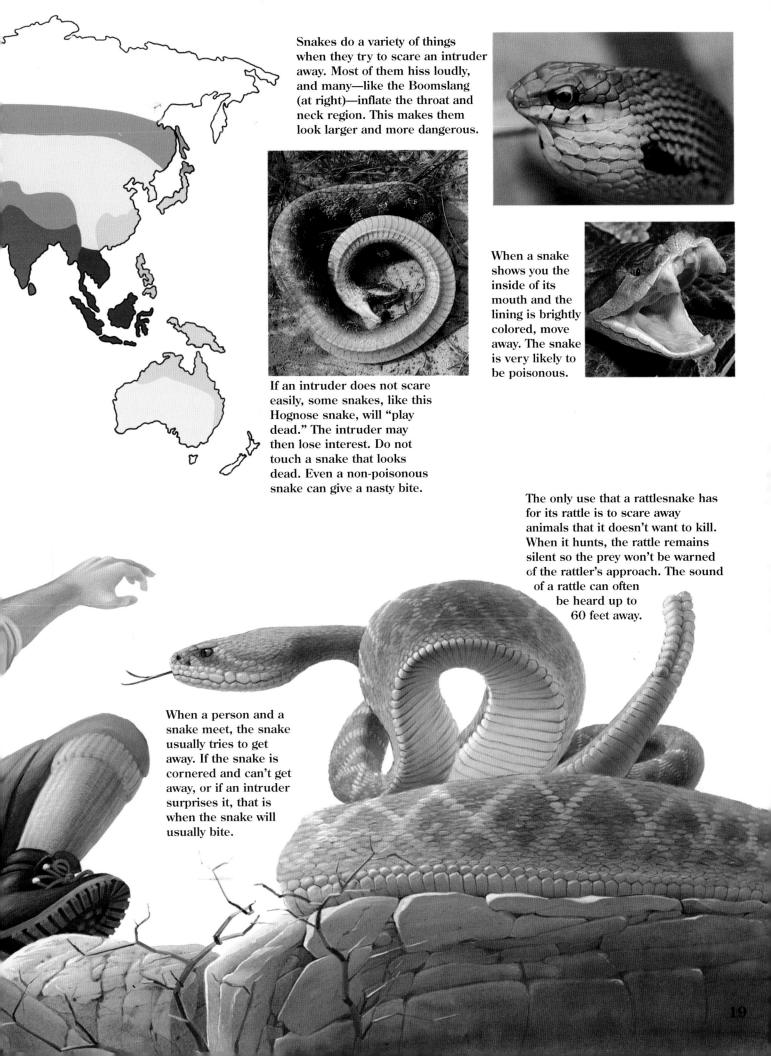

Snake behavior is influenced to a great extent by the weather. Like other reptiles, snakes are cold-blooded. This means the temperature of their bodies depends on the temperature of the air. Among other things, air temperature determines where snakes can live, when they will be active, and when they will mate. In general, snakes are most comfortable in temperatures between 70 and 99 degrees Fahrenheit. If the temperature falls below 39 degrees or rises above 100 degrees, most snakes will die.

When the air is chilly, snakes often bask in the sun. This raises their body temperatures above the temperature of the surrounding air. In hot weather, they often bury themselves in sand or hide under a bush or a rock to lower body temperature.

Finding a place to keep warm when the weather gets cold can be a life-and-death matter for a snake. Many snakes "hole up" for the winter in caves, with other snakes of their own kind. Hundreds of snakes may occupy the same den. During the rest of the year, snakes usually live alone.

As the weather aboveground gets colder, the snakes in the den hibernate. They become lethargic and may even appear to be dead. When warm weather returns, they revive and leave the den in search of food. Spring is also the time when most snakes look for mates.

Scientific experiments show that there is a wide range of variation in the temperatures that snakes from different climates prefer. Snakes from colder climates feel most comfortable in temperatures that are a full 15 degrees Fahrenheit cooler than temperatures preferred by snakes from desert climates.

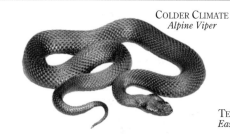

COLDER CLIMATE
Alpine Viper

TEMPERATE CLIMATE
Eastern Hognose Snake

Some snakes give birth to live young. Snakes that reproduce in this way are called *ovoviviparous*. The unborn young are in thin casings, or sacs, inside the mother. They hatch from these egg sacs just before or immediately after emerging from their mother. Rattlesnakes are ovoviviparous.

Combat "dances" are performed by some types of male snakes. They rear up, twist around, and try to knock the other snake to the ground. Usually, neither snake is hurt. The dance has nothing to do with courtship as was once thought.

Most snakes are *oviparous*. They lay eggs, from which the young later hatch. To protect the babies inside them, the eggs are tough and leathery, and the young snakes sometimes have a difficult time breaking out of them. Each baby snake has a sharp bump, called an egg tooth, on top of its snout. This helps the young to cut through the shell.

Female snakes leave scent trails to help males find them. When mating, the two snakes may wrap their tails together.

SUBTROPICAL CLIMATE
Cottonmouth

TROPICAL FOREST CLIMATE
Malaysian Short Python

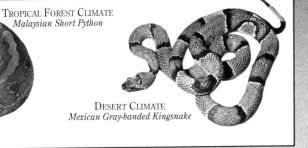

DESERT CLIMATE
Mexican Gray-banded Kingsnake

In ancient Egypt, snake gods were thought to have the power of life and death. To show that they had the same kind of power, the rulers of Egypt wore snake images on their crowns. The most famous example of this is the cobra on the sarcophagus of King Tut, shown here.

Scientists "milk" snakes, draining the venom from their fangs and using it to make serums for curing snakebite victims. The venom is also used to make medicines that stop bleeding, prevent blood from clotting, and treat nervous diseases.

Snakes have been worshiped throughout history, partly out of fear and partly out of admiration. The ability of snakes to shed their skins and be "reborn" again and again has caused many people to see them as symbols of life, fertility, and immortality. Other people (because some snakes have the power to kill) see snakes as evil spirits that bring destruction.

Today, we know that most snakes are harmless to man. As a group, snakes benefit mankind by eating rats and crop-destroying pests. But the age-old fear of snakes still lingers. In fact, the fear of snakes may be greater now than ever before, because so many people who live in cities never get to see many snakes or to learn about them. Our ancestors had the good sense to treat poisonous snakes with a healthy respect, but also to recognize that all snakes are marvelous creatures. We should learn to do the same.

For thousands of years, snakes have been part of rituals intended to ensure the fertility of crops. This picture of a medicine man performing a snake dance was painted on a cave wall in Utah more than 2,000 years ago.

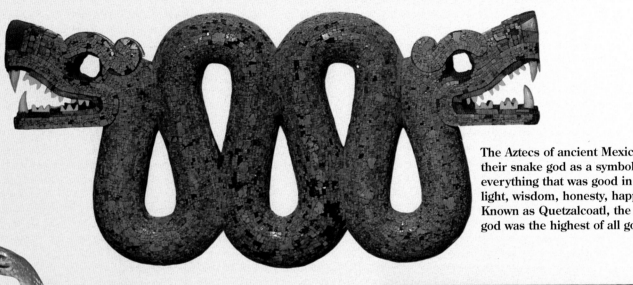

The Aztecs of ancient Mexico saw their snake god as a symbol of everything that was good in life—light, wisdom, honesty, happiness. Known as Quetzalcoatl, the snake god was the highest of all gods.

Although snake charmers seem to risk their lives with deadly snakes, they usually take certain precautions. Snakes are often cooled on ice before a performance, in order to make them sluggish. Fangs may also be removed, or the charmer may sit just beyond the snake's striking distance.

The staff of Asklepios, the ancient Greek god of healing, is still the symbol of doctors today. The snake wrapped around the staff stands for good health and long life.

Index